While the Meter was Running

Marcel Lefebvre

PROVIDENCE ROAD PRESS INC.

Publisher	Dianne Stine Thomas
President	Kirk Thompson
Editor	Eileen McKeever
Art Director	Kate McDonnell
Author	Marcel Lefebvre
Cover Illustration	Ronald DuRepos
Line Illustrations	Janice Friis
Production Manager	Peter Lazanis
Production	Don MacDonald
	Donna Lewzey
	Sharon Telfer
Printing	Data Resolutions

Providence Road Press Inc.
338C Somerset Street West
Ottawa, Ontario K2P 0J9
(613) 567-6330

WHILE THE METER WAS RUNNING
Copyright ©1995 by
Providence Road Press

All rights reserved. Printed in Canada. No part of this book may be used or reproduced in any manner whatsoever without written permission from the publisher, except in the case of brief quotations embodied in critical articles or reviews. For information, address Providence Road Press, 338C Somerset Street West, Ottawa, Ontario K2P 0J9

Canadian Cataloguing in Publication Data

While the Meter was Running

ISBN 1-896243-04-5
Printed and bound in Canada

While the Meter was Running

Marcel Lefebvre

Providence Road Press, Ottawa

To my daughter Lynne and my son John,
whom I love very much.

Table of Contents

Foreword 7
On Taxiology 8
The Judge 9
Sunbeam in the Snow 10
The Old Cowboy 11
Heavenly Dream 12
Ladder Days 14
Politics 15
Three-Column Winner 16
The Hooker and her Friend 18
Smart Kid 19
The Proudest Moment 20
Lester B. Pearson 22
Good Mechanic 23
National Arts Centre 24
Big Spender 26
Hard Twenty 27
Mr. Diefenbaker 28
Mind Over Matter 29
Magic Trunk 30
Heaven 31
Midnight Rendezvous 32
Brian's Embarrassment 33
Big Tears 34

Lost Composure 36
The Drunk 37
Standing Ovation 38
Lorne Greene 40
Generation Gap 41
Gerry Sullivan 42
School Bully 44
Ground Pocket 45
Wine and Cheese 46
Newfie Joke on Me 48
First Proposition 50
Joe Feller 51
Burl Ives 52
Long Way Around 54
Wants and Needs 55
Works of Art 56
Stephen Lewis 58
Santa 59
Customers 60
Cold Love 61
Young Gentleman 62
The Mainlander 64
Tips on Drivers 65
My Favourite Legend 66

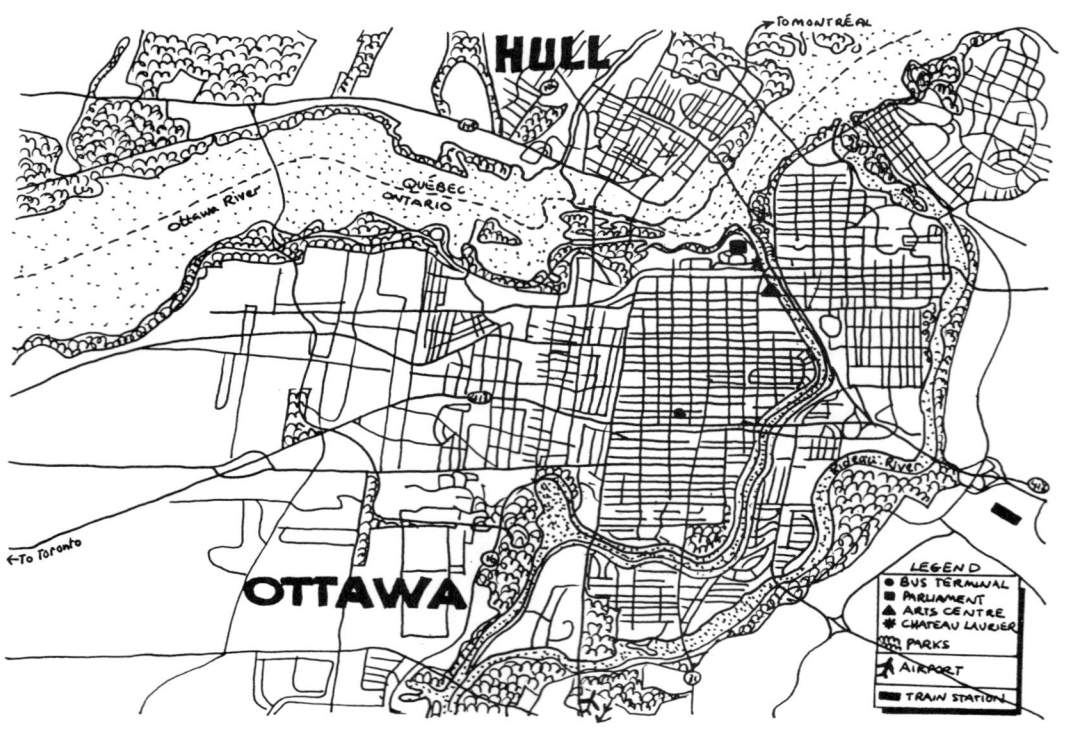

FOREWORD

Come to Ottawa! Our city is the finest in the world—more than one seasoned traveller has told me that.

First of all, Ottawa's beautiful, and filled with waterways. If you come in summer, you'll find flowers, outdoor cafés and festivals of all kinds. In winter, many taxi customers have come for Winterlude. I've never gotten tired of watching the thousands of skaters, young and old, on our 202-km Canal. (When they get tired, they stop for hot chocolate and beaver tails—something you don't want to miss!) There are so many things to see and do, and some of the finest restaurants anywhere.

If you're married, bring your family; if you're single, bring your friends. By the way, if you're a man, you might be interested in this: They say that women here outnumber the men, four to one (although somebody is probably out there having fun with my other three because I only have one.)

You'll enjoy every season, that's for sure, and here are my personal favourites: the Tulip Festival in Spring, the Jazz Festival in Summer, autumn colours in the Gatineau Hills, and Winterlude's ice-sculpting competition. No matter where you live, come and see and enjoy Ottawa. And if anyone asks, tell them Marcel sent you.

Marcel

ON TAXIOLOGY

If a psycho can become a psychologist, why can't a taxi driver become a taxiologist? I think I coined that word.

I drove some people to the airport one day. I was talking to the guy in the front and one guy in the back said, "Listen to my friend; he's a doctor." And I said, "So am I." That sure got their attention.

He said, "What kind of a doctor are you?" I told him that I had a doctorate in taxiology and he said, "What's that?" and I told him that I was a cross between a psychiatrist and a transportation engineer, and that made me a taxiologist. They called me doctor all the way to the airport.

I got my doctorate from the Ottawa University of hard knocks. I tell you a guy can have fun driving a taxi.

THE JUDGE

The sign said *NO U TURN from 4 to 6 p.m.* I looked at my watch and it said one minute to 4:00. I made the turn.

Before you could say whatever-the-hell-you-say-at-a-time-like-that the police officer stopped me and started writing out a ticket. You see, his watch was one minute ahead of mine.

This ticket meant lost points and a $20 fine, so I decided to fight it in court. The judge said, "Guilty as charged." Well, life is hard on taxi drivers, especially in court.

I went back to work and picked up a fare going to the airport. I just had to get the court injustice off my chest, so I told my passenger all about it. I felt better already.

When we got to the airport, my passenger paid the fare and gave me an extra $20 bill. I said, "I can't take this," and he said, "That's all right, son, I'm a judge from Vancouver and I find you not guilty." He refused to take back the $20. Now doesn't that restore your faith in humanity? Thanks again, Judge!

SUNBEAM IN THE SNOW

Now you wouldn't think that a sunbeam could be hidden in a snowbank. Well you're wrong. It happened when I was on my way to pick up a fare on Renfrew Avenue.

It was snowing hard. It was late at night and I was having a hard time seeing the house numbers. All of a sudden I hit a snowbank. In the snowbank there was a small, white car — a sunbeam. In the car there was a couple smooching; well it scared the hell out of all of us. Although there was no damage to the cars, I'm sure there must have been a small dent in the romance.

THE OLD COWBOY

His name was Bill, and he must have been 80 years old when I used to drive him to the Good Companion Club on Albert Street. This was in the late sixties or early seventies. I always looked forward to driving him because he had been a real cowboy in his younger days and he still was at heart. He still had his cowboy hat, and he wore it all the time.

I had been into western comic books in my youth, so we always had a lot to talk about. One day while driving him I said, "I've heard some rumours about you," and he looked around with a twinkle in his eye and asked what the rumour was. I told him that I had heard that he'd gotten three old ladies in the family way at the Club. He looked at me real serious and said, "That's a damn lie—I just danced with them." He really wanted to know who had started that rumour and I wasn't about to tell him that it was me. I kept on teasing him about that and he kept on denying it.

That old cowboy must be in that big ranch in the sky by now, and he's probably the top hand too. If you are, Bill, keep a horse saddled for me.

HEAVENLY DREAM

I was pulling into the Chateau Laurier Hotel and I could see all these women dressed in white coming out of the hotel. And there were a lot of men dressed in black. I parked my cab to wait my turn and they just kept coming out ... I mean a lot, by the tens and twenties. What a beautiful sight; they kept coming out until I could hardly stand it any more.

I thought that I had died and gone to heaven, with all these white angels going by. I walked over and stopped one, and asked her if indeed they were angels and if I was in heaven. She started to laugh and said, "No, we're the Mormon Tabernacle Choir, all three hundred and thirty of us."
They were performing at the Arts Centre that night.
Did that ever bring me back to earth. And the truth is,
I liked earth all the more for it.

LADDER DAYS

I dreamed I was going to heaven. It was a long way up, and I had to climb the ladder. The only catch was, on the way up, I had to write all my sins on each step of the ladder. I had with me a big, big piece of chalk.

Well I started writing. And writing. And writing. And writing. This was one hell of a job.

When I had gotten about half way up, I felt someone stepping on my fingers. I looked up and saw Brian Mulroney; he was on his way down. "Where are you going?" I asked him. He told me that he was going down for more chalk.

POLITICS

I have rubbed elbows with so many politicians—mostly while getting their luggage out of the trunk—that I think I'm qualified to comment on them. I tell you, contrary to popular belief, they are a hard-working bunch of people. Taxi drivers have long hours, and so do politicians. I've driven politicians to work early in the morning, then returned to drive them back home late at night.

I gather that most of them come to Ottawa with dreams of grandeur, then later find that it's impossible to do all that they set out to do. Most of them get their dream bubble burst, but they go on to do the best that they can, anyway.

Whether you're a politician or a taxi driver, the best policy for dealing with the public is to stay neutral. I don't understand all this left-wing, right-wing stuff. I always thought that I was middle-of-the-road, but the police don't take it too kindly if you drive in the middle of the road. So here in Canada we drive on the right side. Does that make me right wing?

THREE-COLUMN WINNER

Somehow, over the years, these three stories about me got into Dave Brown's column in the Ottawa *Citizen*.

1. A secretary got in my cab one day, and after giving me her destination, said that she had just had a beautiful lunch. She had been named the secretary of the month. Anyway, she felt real good, and I decided to help her day along even more. When we got to the place she was going, I said, "This trip is compliments of Diamond Taxi." (That's who I drove for at the time.) I told her to always remember that diamonds are a girl's best friend. If you think she felt good before, you should have seen her then.

2. When I was driving for Modern Taxi this kid about ten years old had missed his stop at the Civic Hospital. When he got to the bus station he didn't have enough money to take a taxi to the hospital. After asking other drivers to take him, and being refused, he finally got to me. I had a son his age, so it was my duty to see that he got to where he was going. After all, he only had a little money and I just felt like not charging him. He was a nice kid.

3. There was a time, in the summer, when I used to write U.S. license plate numbers. I had a list of all the states, and when I saw a state that I didn't have I would jot down the number. One year (by that time, I think I had about 30 states), at Christmas I wanted to pick a plate number out of a hat and send its owner a Christmas card, along with five dollars to thank them for visiting Canada. I tried to get the name corresponding to the plate number, but I was never able to. So much for that good tourism idea.

THE HOOKER AND HER FRIEND

One night I was sent to a certain address, and out came a woman whom I recognized to be a local hooker. She asked me to take her to a hotel nearby.

When we got there, she said that she had no money, but that one of her boyfriends was inside, and she would send him out to pay me. I waited for a few moments, then out came this guy who looked familiar. He paid me and left. He had me puzzled for awhile, until I realized the reason I had not recognized him: The last time I saw him he had a white collar on, and was preaching about the evils of prostitution.

Maybe it's only my imagination, but I'm sure I once heard it said that you should practice what you preach. But, come to think of it, maybe he *was* only practicing what he preached!

SMART KID

Seeing that Johnny Carson never called me to perform on his show, I did my entertaining in my cab. While driving this nice couple to a restaurant, I was telling them about a guy who had a smart son. He told his wife, "You know, I just can't get over how smart that son of mine is. He's so smart I think he has my intelligence." His wife said, "He probably does, because I still have mine."

The lady seemed to get a bigger kick out of that story than her husband. When I got out and opened her door, she kissed me on the cheek and said, "Thanks, I needed that."

THE PROUDEST MOMENT

I was driving a nice young couple home on a Sunday night. I could hear them counting their meager fortune in French.

She said, *"Combien d'argent as-tu?"* (How much money do you have?)

He said, *"J'ai seulement un dollar vingt-cinq – toi, combien te reste-t-il?"* (I only have $1.25—how much do you have left?)

She said, *"Environ quatre-vingt-dix sous. Le taxi coûtera près d'un dollar cinquante, et nous avons besoin d'une pinte de lait et du pain."* (About 90¢, the taxi is going to cost about $1.50, and we need a quart of milk and some bread.)

I thought this was pretty sad. They didn't know that I could speak French and that I had overheard their conversation. When we got to their door I said, "Congratulations," and they asked what for? I told them that every Sunday night I drove one fare free, and that they were that fare.

Well, you would have thought that they had won a million dollars. When I drove away from there I had a lump in my throat, and I thought my heart was going to burst with pride. Just think, a measly $1.50 could bring so much happiness. In 25 years of taxi-driving, it was my proudest moment.

Just to show you how, in life, what goes around comes around, the very next fare was around $5.00. The passenger gave me a ten and said, "Keep the change." It all comes back—the more you give the more you receive.

LESTER B. PEARSON

To my mind, this Prime Minister was a rare jewel in humanity. While I was driving him one day, we were deep in discussion. When Mr. Pearson found out that I had only a grade five education, he said, "Why don't you go to night school?"

I said that I would probably be thirty by the time I finished. He looked at me with that smile of his and said, "How old will you be at that time if you don't go to night school?"

What the hell can you say to that? I went to night school all right, and I'll always be grateful for that question that day. Isn't it amazing how one unexpected little moment can change your life?

GOOD MECHANIC

Every now and then, when I was sent to pick up a fare, it turned out to be someone I knew. One day, the customers were my car mechanic and his wife; they were going to the bus station.

We started to talk about my car problems, so he said, "Let me drive it the rest of the way, and I'll tell you what's wrong with it." You should have seen the faces on the other drivers at the bus station, when they saw me sitting in the back with the mechanic's wife. He even got out to open the door for us.

NATIONAL ARTS CENTRE

The NAC cost $44 million to build, and I thought it was beautiful. I was really glad to be a taxi driver when we were the first to be invited for a tour—we were the ones who were going to bring many of the people there and drive them home. What a day—I was even interviewed on TV. At the time the population of Canada was about 22 million, and being a wizard at mathematics, I figured that the Arts Centre had cost us $2.00 each.

About two years later I was driving a guy from Vancouver, and he kept going on and on about what a waste of money "that damn Arts Centre" was, and how ugly it was, too. It doesn't happen often, but there are times when I get angry, and this was one of them. I took $2.00 out of my pocket, gave it to the customer, and told him to keep his damn mouth shut, that I was buying out his share. He never said another word about my Arts Centre. And as far as I know, I'm the only proud Canadian who owns two shares.

BIG SPENDER

One morning at the bus station a man got in my cab and gave me directions to where he wanted to go. Then he proceeded to give me hell all the way.

Fortunately I am in a good mood 99% of the time. When they give me hell, it goes in one ear and out the other. Some say that's because there's nothing in the middle to stop it. I let that guy's comments go in and out, too.

Anyway, to get back to the story, when we got to the other end, he pulled out a large roll of bills, with a $100 bill on the top. I could see a lot of small bills. He said sarcastically, "Can you change this?" I grabbed it and said, "Yes sir!" (My wife had given me the mortgage money that morning to deposit.)

I pulled out my roll—with a lot of ones and twos—it was considerably larger than his. He said, "I was just kidding, I have some smaller bills. Give me back my $100." I politely said, "fuddle duddle" and proceeded to give him $96 in ones and twos.

I didn't pay the mortgage for two days so that I could show my $100 bill to the boys and tell them the story. Boy did that feel good, and for a long time, too! Unfortunately I couldn't afford to frame it at the time. As a matter of fact, I still can't afford it.

HARD TWENTY

A friend of mine got a fare out of town to Cumberland. The customer was three sheets to the wind and drowsy. He had a twenty-dollar bill sticking out of his breast pocket. My friend tried to get it, but every time he tried, the guy moved a little. My friend said he must have tried at least five times to get that twenty. Anyway, when they got to the destination, the customer paid him and got out. He leaned back into the car with a grin and said, "You know, driver, this twenty is fastened on the inside with a safety pin."

MR. DIEFENBAKER

I never liked him until I met him. I was sent to the House of Commons one day to pick up former Prime Minister John Diefenbaker. When you drive someone you don't like, the prospects of the trip don't leave much to be desired, but on the way to his home I found him very pleasant. We talked about all sorts of things, mostly about his dog.

When we got to the St. Patrick Street Bridge, about a mile from his home, he asked me to stop. He said that if I would take his briefcase home, he would walk the rest of the way for exercise. He gave me the address, paid me, and away he went. What I didn't know at the time is that Lansdowne, where he lived, was split in the middle, and had a north and a south end.

With my good sense of direction I proceeded to go to the wrong end and got thoroughly lost for a while until the dispatcher got me back on track. I finally got to Mr. Diefenbaker's home as he was walking up the driveway. Well, he got the biggest kick out of that episode, saying that here he was, an old man, and that he had beat me home.

After I got over my embarrassment and apologized, he brought me inside to meet his wife and his dog. I drove him many times after that, but that's the day I got to like the Chief.

MIND OVER MATTER

If I were to get angry at everything that happened on the road each day, I'd have been a raving maniac every night. My passengers used to ask me where I got the patience to drive 12 hours a day in this traffic. I told them, "When someone cuts me off or does something to me, it's all mind over matter: I don't mind and they don't matter." Maybe that sounds crazy, but it sure kept me from going insane!

MAGIC TRUNK

A lady and her little boy were waiting when I got there to pick them up. They had a lot of parcels and stuff, so I pressed the automatic trunk-release button and got out. The little boy, about six or seven years old, asked me, "How did that trunk open?" I looked him straight in the eye and told him that it was a magic trunk, and that "all I do is snap my finger and it opens."

The little boy said, "Do you think that I could do it, too?" I told him to wait until we got to where they were going, and that I would let him try. Boy, was he ever anxious.

When we got there he snapped his fingers and I pressed the button. The trunk opened, his mouth opened, his eyes opened wide, and he just couldn't believe that he had done it. I got all the stuff out, closed the trunk, and the lady paid me. When I got back in, I looked in the mirror and saw him snapping his little fingers. I pressed the button, got out and scolded him for doing that.

I drove off, and half a block away I could see his hand in the air. I just had to press the magic button again. I got out and started shaking my fist at him. By this time they were both doubled over laughing. Kids can sure make your day.

HEAVEN

A priest went to heaven. He was met by St. Peter, who asked, "What have you done to gain heaven?" The priest replied that he had been a good priest and had helped many people in need. St. Peter said, "You are most welcome. Go and sit in the last row."

"But," protested the priest, "why should I have to sit in the last row when that taxi driver is sitting in the front row?"

"Simple," said St. Peter. "Taxi drivers are special. They have been scaring the Hell out of people for years."

MIDNIGHT RENDEZVOUS

I picked up a passenger at the train station. He was straight out of the bush—a lumberjack. He told me that he didn't get to the city too often, so he asked me to take him to a hotel in the Market.

On the way he pulled out a roll of bills big enough to choke a horse, and said, "Here, you keep this for me and pick me up at midnight at the hotel." At midnight I was in front of the hotel.

He came out at 12:20 and I drove him where he wanted to go. I gave him back his money and said, "You sure took a big chance giving me all that money."

He said, with a drunken smile, "The last time I came here I got rolled and woke up broke. I thought I had a better chance with you." He paid me and gave me a $100 tip.

Incidentally, there was $1,800 in that roll, and to this day I feel good about being there at the midnight rendezvous.

BRIAN'S EMBARRASSMENT

The day John Turner won the Liberal leadership was a memorable one for Brian, the doorman at the Chateau Laurier Hotel.

I drove Mr. Turner to the Chateau Laurier where Brian opened the door and said, "Congratulations, Mr. Mulroney." Mr. Turner looked at Brian's name tag and said, "I can understand you making that mistake with a name like yours." Brian is probably still embarrassed to this day.

BIG TEARS

A long time ago I picked up two guys in the Market. The one in front was big, and I mean *big*— about six feet five inches tall and weighing about 275 pounds. The one in the back was about four feet tall and skinny. They wanted to go to Slater and Lyon Streets.

There was a parade on Rideau Street, so I suggested that I had better go around to avoid it. The little fellow in the back scrunched up his face and said, "No. You're not taking us for a ride. I want to go by Sussex." I took his route, and we got stuck in the parade. The little fellow got mad, and gave me hell all the way. He said he was going to kick the hell out of me when we got to his destination.

As it happened, I had borrowed a car that morning because mine was in the garage for repairs. The one I borrowed had a broken seat on the driver's side, and I was sitting low to the floor. So my passenger thought that I was as small as him. His big friend could see me down there and kept telling him to "shut up!"

We finally got there, and the little fellow jumped out and said, "You get the hell out of that car." When I got out his nose was just above my belt. He looked up at me and said, "forget it." I looked over at his big friend, and he was leaning on the top of the car, laughing, with big tears rolling down his cheeks.

As for the little guy, you should have seen the look on his face. It made my day.

LOST COMPOSURE

A small sophisticated lady with a British accent asked in a very shrill voice, "Could you please get me to the train station? I only have five minutes to catch my train." I'm always eager to please a customer, especially when they're pretty. So I said I'd do my best, and I did.

Just before you get to the station there are a few snake-like curves. About half way through, this little British voice in the back exclaimed, "For BLEEP-sake, slow down, I'd rather miss the train!" Before I got over the shock we were there and she did catch her train after all. Funny the little incidents that stick with you for years—I think of her every time I go to the station.

THE DRUNK

Maybe I shouldn't call him a drunk . . . maybe it was the first time he'd had one too many. Anyway, three guys came down the street helping to navigate this other fellow. They poured him in the front seat and said, "Take him home." I took off and asked him where he lived, but he couldn't talk, at least not coherently. I managed to get the street name, which I won't mention because it is a nice small street in the west end of the city.

I got him to the street after holding on to him with one hand because he tried to jump out on the Queensway three times. I could not get his house number out of him so I stopped at houses all along the street and asked each woman to come and see if it was her husband that I had. I got lucky on the fourth house, and the lady helped me carry him in.

There are a lot of people out there who have one too many. I wish they wouldn't.

STANDING OVATION

Monday night of a long weekend, when people are returning to the city, can be one of the most hectic times at the bus station, airport and train station. On such a night in the spring, when everything was slushy, I pulled into the train station. There were at least a hundred people waiting for a cab. They were lined up fifty feet long and ten feet deep. Now, when you're a taxi driver, that really makes you feel wanted.

Although I came from a family with few material things, my parents taught me to be polite and honest, and to respect my elders. To my mind, you just can't have a better inheritance than that. So when I saw an elderly lady with a cane in the middle of the crowd, I stopped my cab in front of her and got out to give her a hand.

By the time I got around the car the lady had her hand on the door handle. Before I could get to her, this big, 40-year-old, well-dressed, ignorant S.O.B. slapped her hand off the door handle, opened the door and climbed in head first. The poor woman almost fell. I got a little angry, to say the least.

I reached just in time to grab him by the back of the collar, and I yanked him out. He fell backward into the slush. The woman got in, some people applauded and we drove away happy. The guy was still down in the slush, and I hope he never gets a cab.

LORNE GREENE

When Mr. Greene got into my cab the hair was just standing on my arms. What a thrill—wow, Mr. Cartwright in person! I told him that I had once driven Dan Blocker and he said that Dan Blocker had been one of the finest men he had ever known.

Mr. Greene asked me to drive him to Lisgar Collegiate for a reunion, and I was so excited I didn't even charge him. He shook my hand and thanked me. He didn't have a big "S" on his chest, but he was a super man in my book.

GENERATION GAP

The three of them came out of the bus terminal door at the same time. There was a well-dressed man, about 40; a beautiful well-dressed woman, about 35; and an elderly lady, 65 or so, a little on the shabby side. How was I to know they weren't together?

I said, "Taxi, sir?" He said, "Yes." So I took the beautiful lady's suitcase and the elderly lady's suitcase. The guy got angry and said, "That old lady is not with us." Me and my big mouth—I couldn't help but say, "I'm sorry, sir. I thought that you were with your wife and daughter."

His wife had the most beautiful smile on her face at that point, and he never said another word all the way to the hotel. He paid me without a tip. But when he wasn't looking, his wife winked and slipped me a five-dollar bill.

GERRY SULLIVAN

I liked him the first time I had the good fortune to meet him. He asked me to take him to Sorento's Restaurant on Gilmour and Elgin Streets. As we arrived there, he asked me if I'd had dinner yet. I said, "Yes, but that was at noon." He laughed, and said that he called the evening meal dinner and at noon he had lunch. So I explained to him that for me it was breakfast, dinner and supper at night, and that I never missed lunch—I had that before I went to bed. He asked me to join him, and I did.

Gerry "Nine-Fingers" Sullivan was a Voyageur bus driver from Toronto. They called him "Nine-Fingers" Sullivan because there was another Gerry Sullivan working for the company. My friend had lost a finger somewhere in his adventures.

Gerry was funny, and fun to be with. That first night I ordered a beer; Gerry ordered a boiler-maker—that was his favourite drink after a 450-mile drive. We told stories, teased the waitress, smoked cigars, and had one hell of a good time. His birthday was on the 12th of April and mine was on the 11th, only twenty years apart. I was about 5 foot 10; he was about 5 foot 20. He was a *big* man.

One year my wife and I had the pleasure of spending a weekend with Gerry and his new bride, Vera, at their home in Toronto. We were treated like a king and queen. They wanted to show us their beautiful city, especially the big needle. Gerry said the best way to see Toronto was by trolley, and we must have been on every damn trolley in town.

Then he said it was time for the big needle—the Beautiful CN Tower—and he made me go to the top. As I recall, it was about half way to heaven, and scarier than hell. Then, as if that weren't all, he said he was taking us to a scary movie. It couldn't be any scarier than going to the top of that needle, I said to myself. We waited in line for 45 minutes, and I said, "This movie must be something if we have to wait this long." He laughed and said that it was unforgettable.

We finally got in, sat down, and "North of Superior" flashed on a big, BIG screen. It was the most frightening thing I'd ever seen. We were holding onto the arms of our seats for dear life, and I thought Toronto was having an earthquake. I guess now it seems like no big deal to most people, but it was my introduction to the Cinemax theatre.

You don't have to be a politician or a celebrity to be in my book. As a matter of fact, this book is not even big enough to tell you about Gerry's qualities. For about five years, until he retired, Gerry and I had supper together every Wednesday night around 9:30. What a fine man and a good friend. I miss him a lot.

SCHOOL BULLY

Do you remember Charles Atlas and his advertisement with the 98-pound weakling? Well, he must have found my picture as a youngster, and used it. That's just about the size I was in school, and moving to a new school every six months or so didn't help matters any. It seemed that every school I went to had a bully that was only too happy to kick the hell out of me.

One night I was dispatched to a call at a lower-town hotel. I spotted my passenger, got out to open the door for him, then recognized him as one of those bullies from days gone by. I don't know what came over me, but I gave him a shot right in the mouth and he fell on his you-know-what. I picked him up and said, "Now we're finally even."

He must have recognized me too because he never said a word. (And maybe the fact that I'd grown to two hundred pounds helped a little.) I then drove him to where he wanted to go. It felt good for a minute, to hit him, but then I realized that what I had just done made me as bad as he was. You just can't win, can you?

GROUND POCKET

In the spring, when everything is melting under the overpasses, there often may be ice in the shade. It was on such a day that I drove a flight crew from the Chateau Laurier Hotel to the airport.

Under an overpass, on a small curve, we hit ice. The car skidded sideways, hit the dry pavement on the other side, and straightened out. The pilot said, "Holy Jesus." I turned to him and said, "Don't worry about that, son—that's just a ground pocket." Well, I tell you, that broke up the whole crew.

WINE AND CHEESE

I heard it announced on the radio. Oh, how I wish that I hadn't. I'm still embarrassed about that night many many years ago, but they say that confession is good for the soul. Nancy Cooper's sexy voice came over the CBC radio station announcing a Wine and Cheese Party and an Art Auction. You see, I'd quit drinking about four months earlier.

One little glass of wine couldn't hurt, I said to myself. I had never been to a Wine and Cheese Party, let alone an Art Auction, so I went. Everything started okay, the cheese was good, the patés, cold cuts and wine. So many, many kinds of wine. I swear that I'm innocent — I didn't know the wine was loaded. When I drank a few too many beers, I would wake up in the morning with a hangover, unable to remember the night before. But with the wine I woke up the next morning with an even bigger hangover and a full recollection of the night before.

It was like a bad dream. When I'm sober I'm kind of shy, but with a few drinks, I'm a pain in the ass like everybody else. I went around shaking hands with everyone telling them how happy I was to meet them, as if they could care less. They must have thought I was a politician! I even had the nerve to shake the hand of Mr. Yousuf Karsh, Canada's most famous photographer. I introduced myself to Mr. Denis Beaulieu, the general manager of the Chateau Laurier, and even to Nancy Cooper—that lovely lady with the sexy voice. I still think of that evening when I see Nancy on the CBC evening news!

NEWFIE JOKE ON ME

I was driving two gentlemen to the airport, and we started telling stories. Newfie jokes were in then, so I came up with two or three and we all had a good laugh. I also told them that I was writing this book, and they said, "Good for you!"

When I was getting their luggage out of the trunk, one of them said, with a big smile on his face, "You should also write in your book that you were telling those Newfie jokes to two Newfies."

Well, it proves my point. I still haven't met a Newfie that I don't like, and the next week I drove two more nice guys from Newfoundland. I later found out that one of them was former Conservative MP John Lundrigan—that famous guy that made Mr. Trudeau say "Fuddle Duddle."

FIRST PROPOSITION

Twenty-one, naïve and shy, first week on the job. The dispatcher sent me to Argyle Avenue, and I managed to find it. Got out of the car, rang the bell, eager to make a good impression on the customer.

The lady came out. She was in her 50s, and God made the poor thing as ugly as possible then hit her in the face with a shovel. But, I reminded myself, she's probably a very nice person. When I opened the back door, she said, "Do you mind if I sit in the front?" Always eager to please, I opened the front door and she got in.

I settled in the driver's seat and, polite as usual, I said, "It's a lovely day, isn't it?" She looked at me and replied, "Yes it is …How would you like a piece of *you-know-what*?" I got red in the face and said, "No thanks. I'm a happily married man, and I want to stay that way." In truth, I was not even going steady at the time.

When you drive a taxi, you're learning something new every day. That first week, I figured out one of my first important lessons: There are some addresses you just never want to go back to again.

JOE FELLER

In my opinion, Joe Feller had the finest men's wear store in Ottawa. For a special occasion, everybody I knew headed to Joe Feller's store to get dressed. You know, they were really good quality clothes. The pair of socks I got there for my wedding day lasted 22 years!

I remember once a friend came to visit and talked about old times. I was telling him that we had held a party the week before, and I was sorry that he had not been able to come. He asked, "Was there anybody there that I know?"

I wanted to impress him, so I told him that the guest list had been huge, and even Joe Feller had been there. Well, he just couldn't believe that he had missed a party with Joe Feller. I never did tell my friend that it wasn't true, but I had an opportunity to drive Mr. Feller to the airport one day, and I told him that story. He got a big laugh out of that.

Too bad he retired and sold the store. After that I just couldn't imagine where my son was going to get his wedding suit.

BURL IVES

When I picked him up at the Chateau Laurier on October 19, 1984, he looked familiar, but I wasn't sure why. Though I had heard his voice often on animated cartoons and on radio, I had not seen him on TV very much, and never before in person.

I hate to bother celebrities—you know, everybody is always after them for autographs and things, and I feel they deserve their privacy. But when his companion called him Burl, and then Mr. Ives, I figured it out. What a thrill! I loved that man and his songs.

They wanted to go shopping, and as I drove I told him a few stories that made him laugh. I told him about the guy who was caught in a flooded area: a boat came along and asked him if he needed any help, but he said, "No thank you. I have faith in the Lord and He is going to save me."

But the water kept rising. He was in the second-story window and another boat came along and asked him the same question. He gave the same answer, and the water kept rising. Finally he was on the roof with water up to his neck. A helicopter came along and asked him if he wanted help. "No," he replied. "I have faith in the Lord, and He is going to save me." The water kept rising, and the man drowned.

When he got to heaven and met the Lord, he asked, "I had so much faith in you and you let me drown—how come?" The Lord replied, "What the hell do you mean, I let you drown? I sent you two boats and a helicopter. What more do you expect?"

Then I drove Mr. Ives to the Arts Centre stage door. He paid me very well, he shook my hand and said, "Thanks for the stories—I'm sure I can use them." I said it was the least that I could do for all the pleasure he had brought my family and me. I love it when life gives you a chance to say thanks in person.

LONG WAY AROUND

When I was young and in my prime, before this taxi business, I was going with a girl in Montreal. One day I took the bus there. From the bus station I took a taxi to her place. It cost $3.95, and I spent a pleasant weekend.

When the time came to leave, I asked her to call a taxi. She said, "Why call a taxi? The bus station is only a block and a half away!" I have always been self-conscious about that, and I can honestly say that I have never gone the long way around with a passenger.

When you take a taxi, give the address of where you want to go, and don't let on that you don't know the way. If the driver asks, "Which way do you want to go?" bluff it. Say, "You're the driver." He will always go the shortest way because he doesn't know whether you know or not.

WANTS AND NEEDS

When you don't have much money, you seem to want a lot of things that you can't afford. When this happens to me, which is quite often, I think of Aristotle—a man who had very few material things. Aristotle would go to the Bazaar and look around. The people would ask him why he was always there, yet never bought anything. He would say, "I'm always so amazed to see so many things that I don't need."

WORKS OF ART

Just sitting at the Chateau waiting for a fare, and along comes this motorcycle towing a car. This makes you look twice, I'll tell you.

Well, you know me ... I had to find out more about this thing; it was a real work of art. As it turns out, it was hand-built by Fernand Roy, who had the body shop at the corner of Scott and Parkdale. When those guys go on motorcycle trips, they sleep in that little car. Fern and his lovely wife Helene had won many trophies displaying their motorcycle and trailer at shows all over the land.

There was another memorable thing about Fern, too. He had his father's wedding band—size 18, would you believe (How would you like a hand like that around your neck?) —with a little replica of his motorcycle inside. What a thing of beauty, a pendant on a big gold chain. And he sure wore it with pride.

What a nice couple. They became very dear friends. You know, it really pays to stick your nose in things sometimes!

STEPHEN LEWIS

I never liked him when he was in politics. He always said that he was for the little guy, but he used words so long that the little guy couldn't understand. I told him that when I drove him from the airport a long time ago. But when he was on my favourite radio program—"Morningside" with Peter Gzowski—I got to like him a lot.

One day, years later, I drove him to the External Affairs Building. I was real proud of him that day: He had just been made Ambassador to the United Nations. I didn't have the heart to tell him that I was the same driver who had given him hell all those years ago. I just wished him lots of luck.

By the way, "Morningside" on CBC Radio—now that's a top-notch program that you shouldn't miss. Where do you think I got all my education anyway?

SANTA

I picked up a nice elderly gentleman from the Chateau Laurier Hotel. I later found out his name was Aldage Whistle. He had long white hair and a beard, and he told me that he had just finished playing Santa for the children of the employees at the Chateau.

About halfway home I diverted his attention and turned off the meter. When we arrived at his home he asked me how much it was. He said, "That meter was on a while ago." I told him that I couldn't understand it either, but that every time there was a Santa in my cab, the meter just magically turned off by itself.

Mr. Whistle was grateful, but I was even more grateful just to have the pleasure of driving him. I later found out that he had worked at the Chateau for over fifty years, and that it was his 18th year playing Santa. Now tell me, how often does a guy get a chance to give something to Santa?

CUSTOMERS

The customer is always right. Right? Wrong! Some customers will call three different taxi companies, then take the first cab that gets there. Some customers will jump out of your car without paying, and run like hell.

One customer did just that to me. About seven years later he got into my cab and rang up a two-dollar fare. He made the mistake of giving me a ten-dollar bill! I took my two dollars, and told him the rest was for the last ride, plus interest. He said that taxi drivers shouldn't have such good memories, and left. Some customers ... forget it. I don't want to write an encyclopedia, I just want to finish *this* book.

COLD LOVE

When I was just newly married I saw my wife bending over, trying to get some meat out of the freezer. I don't know what came over me, but I ran over and made love to her right then and there.

The next Sunday I went to confession. I told the priest what I had done and he asked me if I was married. I said, "Yes."

"I'm sure God will forgive you, my son," he assured me. "Oh thank you, Father," I said. "I sure hope that the people at the meat market feel the same way."

YOUNG GENTLEMAN

From the bus station, I had the pleasure of driving a young boy to Ashbury College in Rockliffe Park. He was dressed in a school uniform, and we had an enjoyable conversation on the way. When we got there I opened the door for him, he took out his wallet and paid me, gave me a dollar tip, and said, "Thank you very much, sir." I was really impressed with this young man's style and manners; he was a real gentleman of the highest class.

It really restores your faith in the younger generation to meet someone like this. I hope he grows up to be Prime Minister some day—he'd make a good one in my book.

THE MAINLANDER

Years ago, when I drove Dave Rinn of CJOH-TV, I just had to tell him a good Newfie joke:

Two Newfies wanted to get work in a gold mine. The first guy went in for his interview, came out and told his friend that there was nothing to it, and that he had the job. The other guy went in and the interviewer asked him if he ever had worked in a gold mine before. He said that he had worked in a mine for 20 years. Then the interviewer asked him if he had his hard hat and his light. The Newfie said, "No." The interviewer looked confused. "I thought you said that you had worked in a mine before," he said. The Newfie nodded. "I did," he replied, "but I always worked the day shift."

Dave laughed, and asked me if I knew why all Newfie jokes were so simple. I had to ask why. He said with a grin that they were simple so we Mainlanders could understand them. He was a young reporter at the time, and even then I knew he would do well—'cause he's a nice guy.

TIPS ON DRIVERS

- Always get into the taxi before stating your destination. That way, if you're not going far enough, the driver can't tell you he's occupied on another call.

- Do be nice to your driver—after all, he's working for a living too. But if he's impolite or rude, report him to the boss, not the dispatcher. (The dispatcher might be his friend!) Better yet, report him to the City License Bureau. We all want good drivers; and chances are if he's not nice to you, he's not nice to others.

- If you leave valuables in a taxi, remember that nearly 90% of drivers will take found objects to the taxi company office. But sometimes we don't even see the item. The next customer gets in, picks it up and keeps it—but we get the blame!

- Regarding tips, some customers do, and some don't, but never tip a bad driver. And who am I to say how much? Anything is usually appreciated. The only thing that is a little frustrating is when an elderly person wants to give you a five-cent tip and takes five minutes to do it. In the meantime, the meter has gone up by 75 cents. As they say, "time is money," but you can't complain when it comes from the heart, can you?

MY FAVOURITE LEGEND

My old nature bible is *The Complete Wilderness Almanac* by Berndt Berglund & Clare E. Bolsby, from Pagurian Press Limited. This book is the cornerstone of my library—with tips on hunting and fishing, cooking game, dressing in the Indian ways, outdoor refrigeration, many other skills and ideas and my favourite, "The Legend of Tommy Whitehawk."

This legend must be carried on for the preservation of mankind, and I only wish that I was like the man described. Well anyway, I am what I am, and at least sometimes I can make people laugh. You try hard in life, and you just never know what'll happen. Who ever would have guessed that I'd write a book? And that I'd get a chance myself to pass on this legend?

THE LEGEND OF TOMMY WHITEHAWK
By Don Inmam

TIME, as we express it here, was not calculated by summers or years, as we do now, but instead was measured by events that became woven into the fabric of the lives of the Indian people and was as much a part of their existence as sunrise and sunset.

One such great event took place long ago. This was when a great chief, Migwakwa Ekowapip (Guardian of the Forest), called all the tribes together to tell them of how he had been visited by the Great Spirit who said to him that all things were brothers—that the Earth and the water and the trees and all things were ONE and each depended upon the other to live. And that man, most favored of all creatures, had the responsibility to guard each and every thing and keep it as it had been created.

All the tribes held council and let it be known that they would indeed follow the great chief in this for they knew that he had been chosen because of his wisdom and his deep understanding of nature.

However, there were those who were jealous of him and treacherously lured him to the edge of a high cliff from which they pushed him to his death.

But he did not die.

As he fell, he suddenly changed into a white hawk and flew deep into the forest out of sight.

Without him men soon forgot his teachings and used the earth and water, and all nature, carelessly and without thought of tomorrow.

The legend says that when a chosen person is born, the hawk will come to him to make it known that he will teach men again that all things are ONE.

Such a bird came to Tommy Whitehawk.

And such a bird can come to me and you.

Acknowledgments

There are many people who have helped me along the road of life, and it would take an entire book to thank them all. Most notably, thanks to my wife, Lucille, for putting up with the millions of times that I asked her how to spell words. Also, for inspiring me to put her in my many stories over the years, whether true or imaginary.

As for my cousin, Philippe Denis, thank you simply for being in my life, for serving as the brother I never had. And thank you for lending us your taxi for the book cover design. I must also note the many taxi drivers over the years (the good ones), for their stories, their camaraderie and for making the profession one I was proud to be part of.

My appreciation also to publisher Dianne Thomas, who has laughed at my stories and believed in me. And finally, thank you—to whomever you thank at a time like this—for my sense of humour. It always has made the path easier to walk ... even the bumpy spots.

Have you ever driven a taxi?

Send your best stories for possible inclusion in our next taxi book to:

Providence Road Press, 338C Somerset Street West,
Ottawa, Ontario, K2P 0J9 Canada

Manuscripts will be acknowledged but cannot be returned.

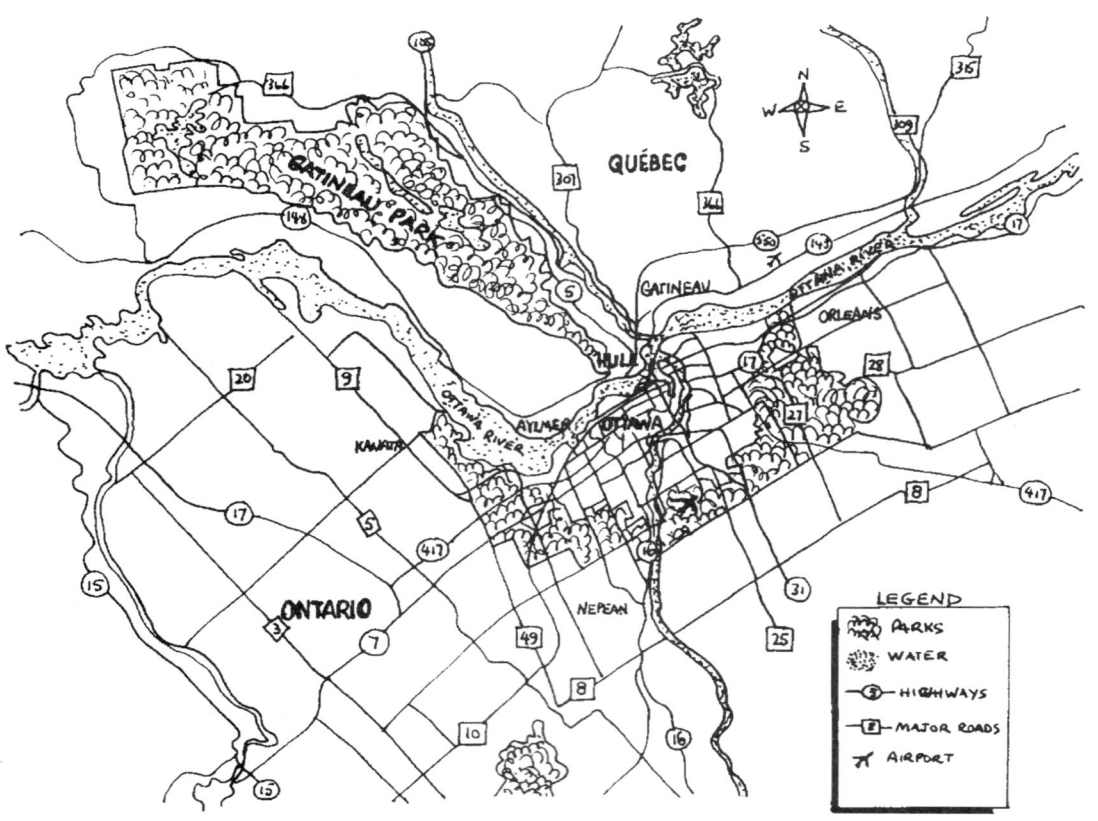